Wisdom Within
by Allison Morgan

Illustrations by Veronique Jolie

Copyright 2014 by Allison Morgan. All images copyright 2014 Allison Morgan
ISBN 978-0-9912843-0-6
Published by Zensational Kids, LLC

All rights reserved. No part of this book may be reproduced in any form by electronic or mechanical means including photocopying, recording, or information storage and retrieval without permission in writing from the author.

The author, illustrator and publisher disclaim any liability or responsibility for any injuries that may result from practicing the yoga poses outlined in this book. This is not intended as an exercise or therapy program. It is recommended that you consult a physician before engaging in a yoga practice to ensure your safety and the safety of the child.

To the 3 most inspiring young women I know,

Mollie, Rachel and Lauren

and to my husband, John, who knows just when to remind me

that I can achieve anything I put my heart into.

A NOTE TO PARENTS, CAREGIVERS AND TEACHERS

It is easy to forget, in the busy-ness of our lives, that we all possess an intuitive wisdom. This knowledge is what helps us navigate our paths to understanding ourselves and our purposes in life. Our main purpose is actually quite simple. It is to be peaceful, joyful and happy. As parents, it is probably the most important thing that we want for our children, for them to be happy. The key to discovering this state is to be happy with who you are. This is accessible to each and every one of us all the time when you learn to listen to the wise voice within you.

In this book, I use nature as an example of how all living parts of this great earth innately know their purpose and easily find happiness. A rabbit does not wish to be a snake. A bird knows that it CAN fly. Monkeys swing through the heights of tall trees without a fear of falling. Children easily connect to the wonders and beauty found in nature, making the characters presented very meaningful. We are all part of nature. Yes, we are also creatures of this planet. Within us, lies this knowledge of insight, purpose and happiness, as well. The greatest difference between humans and the creatures of the earth is that we have this wonderful mind that is constantly feeding us with information (some true, some not so true). How do we listen to our inner quiet, intuitive teacher, when our chatty mind continues to spew out millions of thoughts? How do we discover who we really are when the conversations and thoughts tell us conflicting things?

Over the past 25 years, I have worked with hundreds of children and families to help them discover their inner teacher, building self awareness and self-esteem amidst various physical, emotional, cognitive and social challenges. As an occupational therapist and a yoga instructor, I have found yoga to be one of the most effective tools to help find inner peace, personal strength and intuitive wisdom. In the back of this book, I have provided instructions for guiding your child through some yoga poses, breath and meditation. These fun and engaging activities help to calm the nervous system and relax the body. This assists in quieting our racing mind. When our minds are quiet and clear, the chattiness softens and the wisdom within can be heard. There may be a gentle whisper of, "I am kind. I am joyful. I am loving. I am strong. I am brave." I hope you enjoy sharing this experience with your child. Perhaps you will find your wise teacher within, as well, guiding your bliss and happiness in life.

Many blessings to you all,
Allison

P.S. If you would like to learn more about yoga, and creating more happiness, resilience and awareness in your life and the lives of children, visit our web site www.zensationalkids.com. Join us for a training.

Welcome to this beautiful place. Mother Earth is her name.

She shines with fabulous creatures.
No two are quite the same.

Each living thing is special and has a purpose here.

This knowledge can be tricky, like a whisper in your ear.

Watch how nature understands
the plan for truth and peace.

You will find your secret, too.
Your search should never cease.

Animals, bugs, birds and trees
know just what to do,
to be happy, bright and joyful
while part of nature's crew.

How do they know their places,
and jobs that they perform,
keeping nature balanced
through the sunshine or a storm?

Listen and watch closely
as their talents will unfold.

There are special gifts within us
when we're young and very old.

Spiders spin elaborate webs,
with balanced patterns found.

Is there a weaving class they go to
so the patterns will be round?

A cat can walk a narrow fence,
no safety net below.

Do they practice day and night...

...or to the circus do they go?

Monkeys swing from branch to branch,
and soar between the trees.

No one taught the monkeys this,
but their mommies sure are pleased.

Many dogs can swim across a river or a lake.

Are there special swimming lessons
that these creatures need to take?

Lessons are not needed for the creatures of the earth.

This wisdom is within them
and they know it all from birth.

Baby birds will leave their nest when they are set to fly.

Their mother watches closely to make sure they reach the sky.

Does she push them, does she squawk,
to get them on their way?

Or does something deep within them
let them know...

      TODAY'S THE DAY!

Caterpillars know when a cocoon should take its form.

Bundled, oh, so tightly 'til it's ready to be reborn.

When the time is right, they break out and are free,

Revealing another side of life for all the world to see.

Bears know when it's time to find a cave, dark and warm.

They hibernate, day and night, through the winter storm.

Do alarm clocks ring to welcome spring's arrival?

Listen and awaken. Your slumber time is final.

Bunnies know that they must hop.

Slithering just won't do.

Have you ever seen a bunny walk?

Just like me or you?

Seeds that blossom into trees know which way to grow.

There are no Mom or Daddy trees
to tell them where to go.

They know their roots dive down beneath
the earth, so dark and deep.

Their branches find the sunlight, for nourishment and heat.

All of nature on this earth knows what it must do.

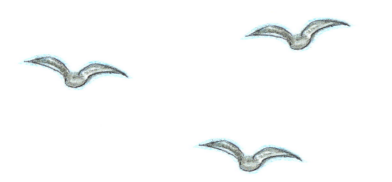

The sun will rise...

the moon will set...

just to name a few.

I am Loving

I am happy

I am Smart

I can do anything.

I AM Peaceful

I am Strong

What do **you** know about yourself
that no one had to teach you?

The answer is simple and already there.
Your heart knows what to do.

There is wisdom deep within
that helps us everyday

To share, be helpful, and be kind,
in every single way.

You entered this world with grace and kindness
flowing through your heart.

You know that bliss begins with you
and is a special part.

We all have teachers deep within
that guide our every move.

You and Spirit work together
to set you in your groove.

In your life there may be times
    you're filled with hurt or sorrow.

But remember...
    Peace and joy are feelings
    that you don't need to borrow.

They are yours...
all the time,
carried in your heart.

Your search should never take you far
and this is where you start...

Close your eyes and breathe in deep.
Notice a peaceful feeling.

Smile bright and shine your light...
each breath, a new beginning.

Dream, hope and imagine

the YOU, you want to see.

Hold on to the vision,

of all you want to be.

Smile and be proud

of exactly who you are.

Your wisdom from within

        will take you very far.

POSES AND BREATH TO RELAX THE BODY, FOCUS THE MIND, AND ADD FUN!

SPIDER

1. Stand with your feet apart.
2. Inhale with your hands together and reach them towards the sky.
3. Exhale and squat down, but don't let your bottom touch the floor.
4. Reach your hands through your legs and place each hand on the floor by the pinky toe of each foot, turning your body into a spider. Now it's time to spin the thread to make your web.
5. Keep your hands and feet on the floor.
6. As you inhale, slightly straighten your legs, but don't lift your hands off the floor.
7. As you exhale, squat down again.
8. As you inhale up and exhale down repeatedly, imagine that you are spinning a silky thread to weave a web.

In the imaginary web of your mind what would you like to catch hold of? A skill perhaps? What would you like to release from that web? Maybe a persistent thought that isn't very kind to you or someone else?

The author, illustrator and publisher disclaim any liability or responsibility for any injuries that may result from practicing the yoga poses outlined in this book. This is not intended as an exercise or therapy program. It is recommended that you consult a physician before engaging in a yoga practice to ensure your safety and the safety of the child.

CAT

1. Come onto your hands and knees.
2. Inhale and make your back flat.
3. Exhale and round your back, lifting the middle of your back towards the sky and your head and hips move toward the earth. Your back will arch like a frightened or angry cat.
4. Inhale to flatten your back. Exhale to round your back.

What makes you scared? What makes you angry?

MONKEY

1. Stand with your feet apart.
2. Inhale one arm forward and the other arm back, behind you. For example, swing your right arm forward and your left arm back.
3. Exhale and switch, swinging your left arm forward and your right arm back.
4. Keep swinging your arms in this alternating pattern. Remember to inhale swinging in one direction, then exhale swinging in the other.
5. Extend your arms as far as you can as you swing, as if you are reaching for a branch far away.

How far can you reach? Can you reach for something in your life and be fearless like the monkey soaring high in the trees?

DOG

1. Come onto your hands and knees.
2. Push your feet and your hands into the floor while lifting your bottom up to the sky.
3. Your body will make the shape of an upside down "V".
4. Pretend there is a tail at the bottom of your spine. Wiggle your hips from side to side to shake that doggie tail.

How does it feel to walk on your hands and feet like a dog? Do things look different from this view? Sometimes it is good to look at things from a different view or perspective.

BIRD

1. Sit or stand in any comfortable position, with your back straight and tall.
2. Inhale and reach your arms out to the side and up over your head. Keep your arms straight, stretching your arms up towards the sky.
3. Exhale, bringing your arms back down to your sides.
4. Repeat, inhaling and lifting your wings toward the sky and exhale, lowering them to your side.
5. Imagine yourself soaring through the clouds.

Where would you like to fly?

BUTTERFLY

1. Take a blanket or a beach towel and lay it on the floor.
2. Lie down across one end of the towel and roll yourself up, making a comfy cocoon. Make sure your head stays out so you can see where you're going.
3. Once you are all wrapped up, wiggle your way out until you are free or roll out.
4. When you change into the butterfly, sit on the floor and place the bottoms of your feet together. Your legs become your lower wings.
5. Take your hands and place them on your shoulders. Your arms become your upper wings.
6. Inhale and open your wings. Exhale and bring them together.

What colors are your wings? Draw a picture of yourself as a butterfly or a dragonfly.

BEAR

1. Come into DOG pose. Turn your hands and feet into giant, strong bear paws.
2. Walk around the room on your hands and feet.
3. Growl and roar like the fiercest bear.

What makes you scared? What makes you mad? Growl and let it go.

BUNNY BREATH

1. Scrunch up your nose and wiggle it a bit like a bunny.
2. Take 4-6 quick, short, breaths in through your nose.
3. Open your mouth and slowly let our all of the air.
4. Repeat this sequence of taking in 4-6 quick, short breaths and exhaling slowly through your mouth.

How many quick breaths in can you take before you feel like letting the air our of your mouth?

TREE

1. Turn yourself into a tiny little seed by kneeling on the floor. Bring your hips to your heels and your forehead to the floor.
2. Imagine that the soil is covering your back to keep you warm and safe.
3. As you inhale, feel the soil against your back. As you exhale, feel your roots start to dive into the earth.
4. Begin to grow your tree slowly. Each inhale reaches your branches closer to the sky. Each exhale reaches your roots into the ground.
5. Once you are standing, bring both palms together at your heart center (like a prayer). This will help you stay centered and balanced.
6. Focus your eyes on something across the room. This is the key to staying balanced as you then begin to slowly lift one leg off the ground.
7. Place the bottom of your lifted foot against the side of your shin, or your inner thigh. Place it wherever it is comfortable for you.
8. Hold your balancing tree pose and count how many slow, full breaths you can take.
9. Just like a strong tree, a gusty wind may come and push you off balance, but your connection to the earth can keep you steady and strong. Don't let the big winds blow you over.

What are some things that make you feel connected, strong and safe?

MEDITATIONS TO SHARE WITH YOUR CHILD

You may begin by reading each step of these meditations to guide your child or read the process and complete the steps on your own. Once you connect to the feeling of each meditation, it may be easier for you to teach them to your child.

"I AM HAPPY" MEDITATION

1. Sit comfortably, or lie quietly on the floor and close your eyes

2. Place you hands on your belly and feel it rise and inflate as you inhale and then become small as you exhale. In yoga, we call this a "belly breath." Do this a few times until you feel the rhythm of your breath.

3. Begin to think of something that makes you very happy. It may be something that you like to do such as baking, coloring, or playing with a special toy, etc. Perhaps it is being with a special person such as a good friend, mom or dad, a grandparent, etc.

4. Continue to see yourself in this "happy" moment and continue your belly breathing.

5. Now, notice how you feel in this moment, doing your "happy" activity. In your mind's eye, are you smiling? Are the people around you smiling too? How does it feel? This is YOU being HAPPY.

6. When we remember the happy times in our lives and become aware of how we feel when we are happy; our mind, body and spirit are able to call upon this feeling whenever we need it. It is a way of "practicing" happiness. We become better at anything that we practice.

"AMAZING ME" MEDITATION

1. Sit comfortably, or lie quietly on the floor and close your eyes.

2. Place your hands on your belly and feel it rise and inflate as you inhale and then become small as you exhale. In yoga, we call this a "belly breath." Do this a few times until you feel the rhythm of your breath.

3. You are going to create a "movie" in your imagination. In this movie, YOU get to be the DIRECTOR and the STAR.

4. The title of the movie is "AMAZING ME." It features you being and doing anything that makes you happy. It can be something you may not have excelled in yet, but hope to in your future. It is like seeing yourself in a wish.

5. Start your film rolling and picture the scene. Where are you? Who is with you? What is it that you are doing? Whatever it is that you wish you can do, in this movie, it is no longer just a wish. It is your reality, here within your imagination. You CAN and you ARE actually achieving all of your dreams in this movie!!!! Dream BIG and dream clear.

6. Breathe into this feeling so that it fills your entire body from head to toe and stretches out beyond your skin and bones and fills up all of the space around you.

7. Picture yourself not only being good at something, but being GREAT at it. Perhaps you are playing basketball. In your movie, you make every basket. You hear people cheering and your heart begins to soar. Imagine yourself dribbling the ball to the basket, setting yourself up and shooting. SWISH and it is IN!!!! Maybe you are an artist. Sketches, paintings, or sculptures, flow from your heart into your hands. Expressing yourself through art relaxes you and fills you with joy. Maybe you hope to achieve a special award, grade or medal in a sport or school or special activity.

8. Believe you can BE and can DO anything you desire. Some of the most famous singers, basketball, baseball players, etc. were not the BEST at what they did when they started, but they believed in themselves THE MOST.

9. Believe you can, and you are on your way.

SPECIAL THANKS

Completing this project would never have happened without the love, encouragement and talent of several people that I am honored to have in my life. To my parents, the lessons in this book were seeds planted by you, thank you. To my niece, your artistic ability is truly a gift. It can lead you anywhere your heart desires. To my mentor and friend Shakta Kaur, your passion for sharing yoga with children has made the future a brighter place. Thank you for teaching me a path to listening to my inner teacher. To my editor, Adarsh Khalsa, thank you for immediately connecting to this story and thoroughly understanding my vision and direction. John Boudreau, without your graphic design finesse and creativity, this book would still be stored somewhere on my computer. I am incredibly grateful to the yogi and yogini models: Allie, Eli, Jacob and to all the children who have opened their hearts, and shared their practice with me.